M. TVLLI CICERONIS
SOMNIVM SCIPINIS

M. TVLLI CICERONIS SOMNIVM SCIPINIS

THE DREAM OF SCIPIO AFRICANUS MINOR,

BEING THE EPILOGUE OF
CICERO'S TREATISE ON POLITY.

TRANSLATED FROM THE ORIGINAL LATIN

BY

W. D. PEARMAN, M.A.
ST PETER'S COLLEGE, CAMBRIDGE,
IIEAD MASTER OF POTSDAM SCHOOL, JAMAICA.

KALPAZ

ISBN: 978-93-5128-724-7(PB)

First Published in 1883
Indian Reprint in 2017

Published by

Kalpaz Publications
C-30, Satyawati Nagar,
Delhi – 110052
E-mail: kalpaz@hotmail.com
Website: kalpazpublications.com
Ph.: +91-9212142040

Cataloging in Publication Data—DK
Courtesy: D.K. Agencies (P) Ltd. <docinfo@dkagencies.com>

Cicero, Marcus Tullius, author.
[Somnium Scipionis. English]
M. Tulli Ciceronis Somnium Scipionis = The dream of Scipio Africanus minor : being the epilogue of Cicero's treatise on polity / translated from the original Latin by W.D. Pearman.
pages cm
"First published in 1883"—Title page verso.
ISBN 9789351287247

1. Scipio Aemilianus, P. Cornelius (Publius Cornelius), Africanus minor, 185 B.C. or 184 B.C.-129 B.C. 2. Scipio, Africanus, approximately 236 B.C.-183 B.C. 3. Conduct of life—Early works to 1800. I. Pearman, W. D., translator. II. Title. III. Title: Dream of Scipio Africanus minor.

PA6304.S7 2017 DDC 129 23

TRANSLATION.

§ 1. WHEN I reached Africa to serve under the general Manius Manilius, being, as you are aware, Military Tribune attached to the 4th Legion, I made nothing of more importance than to meet Masinissa, a prince for good reasons most attached to our family.

As soon as I came to him, the old man folded me in his arms and wept over me; and after some time he looked up to heaven and said: "I give thee thanks, O Sun most high, and you, ye other heavenly beings, for that, before my departure from this life, I behold in my realm and in this my home Publius Cornelius Scipio, by the mere mention of whose name I feel myself made young again: [1]even as the memory of that most excellent and invincible hero is ever present in my heart." After this I asked him about his kingdom and he questioned me about our Commonwealth; and so with much converse on both sides we spent the whole of that day.

§ 2. But in the evening, being right royally entertained, we prolonged our conversation far on into the

[1] Reading *itaque*.

night; the old man talking of nothing but Africanus and calling to mind not only all his deeds but his sayings too.

After this, when we separated for the night, both after my journey and as I had sat up till late at night, sleep folded me in a closer embrace than was usual.

Hereupon there appeared to me,—for my part I believe, out of what we had been talking about: for it often happens that our thoughts and conversations give birth in sleep to some such fancy as that which Ennius records about Homer, of whom, to be sure, in his waking moments he was wont to think and talk very often—there appeared to me Africanus, in that form which was more familiar to me from his picture than from his person. When I recognised him, I shuddered, I assure you, but he said: "Be of good courage and banish fear, my Scipio, and that which I shall say, do thou record.

§ 3. Seest thou yon city, which though forced by my arms to yield obedience to the Roman people, is reviving the recollection of the wars of old and cannot rest in peace,"—now he was showing to me Carthage, from a place on high, full of stars, and bright and shining—, "that city, to attack which thou art now coming almost a private soldier? Within these two years shalt thou destroy it as Consul; and that title, which as yet thou bearest as a heritage from me, shall be won for thee by thine own achievement. But when thou hast rased Carthage, celebrated a triumph, held the office of Censor, and travelled on a mission over Egypt, Syria, Asia Minor and Greece, thou shalt a second time be elected Consul though abroad; and thou shalt bring to its close a most important war, thou shalt utterly destroy

Numantia. But when thou shalt ride in thy car of triumph to the Capitol, thou shalt find the state sorely troubled by the designs of my own grandson.

§ 4. Here, Africanus, must thou display to the fatherland the light of thy courage, genius and wisdom.

But for that time, I see the march of destiny, so to call it, halting between two ways. For, when thy life shall have completed seven times eight full cycles of the sun; and these two numbers, each of which for a different reason is held to be a perfect number, in the revolution of nature shall have fulfilled for thee thy destined sum; to thee alone and to thy name shall the whole community turn together: the Senate, all right-thinking citizens, the allies and the Latins shall fix their eyes on thee; thou shalt be the one man, on whom the community may lean for safety; and, in short, as Dictator thou must needs reorganize the constitution, if only thou shalt escape from the unnatural violence of thy relations."

At this point, Laelius having cried out and all the others groaned exceedingly,— "Hush! please," said Scipio with a gentle smile, "lest you rouse me from my sleep, and hearken a while to the rest."—§ 5. "But still, Africanus, that thou mayest be the readier to defend the Constitution, know this: for all who have preserved their fatherland, furthered it, enriched it, there is in heaven a sure and allotted abode, where they may enjoy an immortality of happiness.

For there is nothing that befalls in the world, more pleasing to that supreme Deity, who governs all the universe, than those gatherings and unions of men allied by common laws, which are called states. From this place do their rulers and guardians set out, and to this place do they return." § 6. Here, although I was greatly terrified, by dread not so much of death as of treachery from men of my own household, I found courage to ask if he was himself alive and my father Paulus and others, whom we regarded as dead. "Yea verily do they live," said he, "who from the bonds of the body, as from a prison-house, have soared away; but your life, as it is called, is really death. Nay, look at Paulus, your father, coming towards you!" On seeing him I shed a flood of tears, but he folded me in his embrace and by kisses endeavoured to hinder me from weeping.

§ 7. And, so soon as I began to be able to speak, having choked back my tears, "Pray, tell me," said I, "most revered and best of fathers, since this is life, as I hear Africanus say, why do I linger on earth? Why do I not haste to come hither to you?" "It is not as you think," said he, "for unless that God, to whom belongs all this region that thou beholdest, shall have discharged thee from the keeping of thy body, the entrance to this place cannot be open to thee. For men were created subject to this law, to keep that globe, which thou seest in the centre of this region and which is called the Earth; and to them a soul was given formed from those everlasting fires, which you mortals call constellations and stars, that round and spherical in form, quickened with divine intelligences complete their orbits and circles with marvellous swiftness. Wherefore, my Publius, thou and all good men must suffer the soul to remain in the keeping of the body, nor without his command, by whom it was given to you, must you leave your human life, lest you should appear to have deserted the post assigned to men by God.

§ 8. But rather, my Scipio, as your [1]grandfather here, as I your sire, follow justice and natural affection, which though great in the case of parents and kinsfolk, is greatest of all in relation to our fatherland. Such is the life that leads to heaven and to this company of those who have now lived their lives and released from their bodies dwell in that place which thou beholdest,"—now that place was a circle conspicuous among the fires of heaven by the surpassing whiteness of its glowing light—"which place you mortals, as you have learned from the Greeks, call the Milky Way." And as I surveyed them from this point, all the other heavenly bodies appeared to be glorious and wonderful,—now the stars were such as we have never seen from this earth; and such was the magnitude of all as we have never dreamed; and the least of them all was that planet, which farthest from the heavenly sphere and nearest to our earth, was shining with borrowed light, but the spheres of the stars easily surpassed the earth in magnitude—already the earth itself appeared to me so small, that it grieved me to think of our empire, with which we cover but a point, as it were, of its surface.

§ 9. And as I gazed upon this more intently, "Pray!" said Africanus, "how long will thy mind be chained to the earth? Dost thou behold into what regions thou art come?

See! the universe is linked together in nine circles or rather spheres; one of which is that of the heavens, the outermost of all, which embraces all the other spheres, the supreme deity, which keeps in and holds

[1] Grandfather by adoption: the younger Scipio was son of Paulus, but adopted by a son of the elder Africanus.

together all the others; and to this are attached those everlasting orbits of the stars. Beneath this there lie seven, which turn backwards with a counter revolution to the heavens; and of these spheres that star holds one, which men on earth call Saturn's star. Next is that bright radiance, rich in hope and healing for the sons of men, which is called Jove's star; then one fiery red and dreaded by the world, which you call Mars; next lower down the sun holds nearly the middle region, the leader, chief and ruler of the other lights, the mind and ordering spirit of the universe, of such magnitude that he illumines the whole and fills it with his light. With him Venus and Mercury keep pace as satellites in their successive spheres; and in the lowest zone of all the moon revolves lighted up by the rays of the sun. Now below these there is nothing more but what is mortal and transient except those souls, which the bounty of the Gods has given to the sons of men; above the moon all is eternal. As for the earth, the ninth and central globe, it does not move but is the lowest point, and towards it all heavy bodies tend by their own gravity."

§ 10. And, as I gazed on these things with amazement, when I recovered myself: "What," I asked, "what is this sound that fills my ears, so loud and sweet?" "This," he replied, "is that sound, which [1]divided in intervals, unequal, indeed, yet still exactly measured in their fixed proportion, is produced by the impetus and movement of the spheres themselves, and blending sharp tones with grave, therewith makes changing symphonies in unvarying harmony. For not only is it impossible that

[1] Reading *disiunctus*.

such vast movements should sweep on in silence; but, by a natural law, the outermost parts on the one side give a grave, and on the other a sharp sound. Wherefore the highest of all, the celestial zone equipped with stars, whose revolution is more swift, moves with a sharp, high note; while this one of the moon, as it is the lowest, with the deepest tone of all. For the earth, which is the ninth, remaining motionless is ever firmly planted in one spot, clinging closely to the centre of the universe. Now the revolutions of those eight spheres, of which two have the same power, produce seven sounds with well-marked intervals; and this number, generally speaking, is the mystic bond of all things in the universe. And learned men by imitating this with stringed instruments and melodies have opened for themselves the way back to this place, even as other men of noble nature, who have followed godlike aims in their life as men.

§ 11. But the ears of men overpowered by the volume of the sound have grown deaf; and you have in you no duller sense than that of hearing; for instance, at the Catadupa as it is called, where the Nile rushes headlong from very high mountains, the tribe which dwells near that spot, owing to the loudness of the noise has lost the sense of hearing. But this sound of the whole universe revolving at the utmost speed is so awful that the ears of men cannot contain it; just as you are unable to look straight at the sun, and your eyesight and its perceptions are overpowered by his rays."

Though marvelling at these wonders I still kept turning my eyes at intervals towards the earth.

§ 12. Thereupon: "I see," said Africanus, "that thou art even now regarding the abode and habitation of mankind. And if this appears to thee as insignificant as it really is, thou wilt ever look up to these celestial things and those of men wilt thou regard not. For what renown among men, or what glory worth the seeking, canst thou acquire? Thou seest that on the earth only scattered and narrow plots are inhabited; while even in the very patches, as it were, in which men dwell, vast deserts are interspersed; and among those who live on the earth, there are not only such breaks that no communication can pass from one set to another, but some live in opposite zones; some on opposite sides of a zone; some even at the opposite point of the earth to you; and from these, at any rate, you can expect no glory.

§ 13. Moreover thou seest that this earth is girdled and surrounded by certain belts, as it were; of which two, the most remote from each other, and which rest upon the poles of the heaven at either end, have become rigid with frost; while that one in the middle, which is also the largest, is scorched by the burning heat of the sun. Two are habitable; of these, that one in the South—men standing in which have their feet planted right opposite to yours—has no connection with your race: moreover this other, in the Northern hemisphere which you inhabit, see in how small a measure it concerns you! For all the earth, which you inhabit, being narrow in the direction of the poles, broader East and West, is a kind of little island surrounded by the waters of that sea, which you on earth call the Atlantic, the Great Sea, the Ocean; and yet though it has such a grand name, see how small it really is!

§ 14. And yet of these very lands, which are frequented and familiar, could thy name or that of any of thy race have climbed beyond the summit of the Caucasus here or crossed the waters of the Ganges there? Who in the other remote regions of the rising or the setting sun or of the North or South will hear thy name? Yet, these cut off, thou seest assuredly in what a narrow field your human glory aspires to range. Again, the very men who talk of you, how long will they talk?

§ 15. Why, even if those generations of men to come should care to hand down, in succession from father to son, the glory of each one of us; yet, still, owing to the deluges and conflagrations of the earth, which must needs happen periodically, we cannot acquire a lasting, much less an eternal renown. Nay, what matters it that mention should be made of thee by those who shall be born hereafter, when there was none among those who were born before thee? who were not fewer in number but were, at any rate, better men; § 16 the more so, as, among those very men, by whom our name may possibly be heard, no one can secure his reputation for a single year. Men, to be sure, commonly measure the year by the return of the sun, that is of a single heavenly body: but when all the constellations together shall have returned to the same point from which they once started; and after long intervals shall have restored the order of the whole heaven as it was before, then can that really be called the year of revolution: in which I hardly dare to say how many generations of men are comprehended. For as at that time, when the soul of Romulus made its way into these heavenly regions, the sun appeared to men to disappear and to be darkened, so whensoever, in the same quarter and at the same time, the sun shall again have been eclipsed, then, all the constellations and stars having been restored to their original position, thou shalt hold that a year has been fulfilled. But of this year know that as yet not a twentieth part hath come round.

§ 17. Wherefore, should'st thou have lost hope of return to this place, on which great and illustrious men rest all their hopes, what then is your human glory worth, which can hardly affect a scanty portion of a single year? Therefore, if thou wilt choose to look aloft and fix thy gaze on this our resting-place and eternal home, nor ever [1]enslave thyself to the rumours of the rabble, nor stake the hope of thy life on the rewards of men: virtue must needs draw thee by her own atttraction to true glory; what others say of thee, let that be their own concern; but still they will talk: however, all that talk of theirs is both confined within those narrow bounds, which thou beholdest, and has never been of long continuance in the case of any: it is buried with the men themselves and ends in the forgetfulness of posterity."

§ 18. When he had ended: "For my part," said I, "Africanus, if indeed for those who have deserved well of their native land a pathway, as it were, is open to the gates of heaven; although from my boyhood treading in my father's footsteps and in thine I have not failed to do you honour, yet now, with so great a prize before me, much more watchfully will I strive." "Strive indeed," said he, "and be persuaded of this: it is not thou that art mortal, but this body: for thou art not that which thy bodily form presents to view, but the mind of any man that is the man, not that figure which can be pointed

[1] Reading *dedideris.*

out by the finger. Know then that thou art a God; since he is a God, who possesses force, feeling, memory and prescience, who directs, governs, and moves that body, of which he is the master, just as much as the supreme God of all moves this universe; and as the universe in some sort perishable is moved by God, who is himself eternal, so is the frail body by an immortal soul.

§ 19. For that which ever moves is eternal; but that which imparts motion to something else and itself receives its motion from some other source, since it admits of an end to its motion must needs have a limit to its life. Therefore that only which moves of itself, as it never abandons itself so it never ceases to move. Moreover this is the source, this is the original cause of motion to all other things that move. Now an original cause has no origin; for all things originate from it, but the original cause itself cannot arise from anything else; for it would not be an original cause if it had originated from something else. And as it has no origin so does it never perish. For if the original cause once perish it will neither be itself reproduced by another nor will it create another from itself; since all things must necessarily spring from the original cause. Hence we see that the original cause of motion resides in that, which is itself self-motive; now that can neither be born nor die; else must the whole heaven and all nature collapse and come to a standstill, nor would it find any power to give it the first impulse of motion.

§ 20. Since therefore it is plain that what is self-motive is eternal, who can deny that this quality is an attribute of our souls? For, whereas everything is soulless, which receives its impulse from without, that, on the contrary, which has a soul, moves by an inward motive of its own. For this is the natural property and essence of the soul; and if this is the only thing in the world that is self-motive, assuredly it has had no beginning but is eternal.

§ 21. This soul do thou exercise in the noblest functions; now the noblest are cares and exertions for our country's weal; and the soul which hath been quickened and trained by these will speed more fleetly to this its resting-place and home. And this will it do the more readily, if even then while still imprisoned in the body, it shall strain beyond it, and surveying that which lies outside it, as much as possible, shall endeavour to withdraw itself from the body. For the souls of those who have given themselves over to the pleasures of the body, and have yielded themselves to be their servants, as it were; and at the prompting of those lusts which wait upon pleasures, have broken the laws of God and man; when they have glided from their bodies, go grovelling over the face of the earth; nor do they return to this place, except after many ages of wandering."

So he departed, and I woke from my dream!